The Exceptional Retail Manager

by
Suresh Banarse

Bloomington, IN  Milton Keynes, UK

AuthorHouse™
1663 Liberty Drive, Suite 200
Bloomington, IN 47403
www.authorhouse.com
Phone: 1-800-839-8640

AuthorHouse™ UK Ltd.
500 Avebury Boulevard
Central Milton Keynes, MK9 2BE
www.authorhouse.co.uk
Phone: 08001974150

© 2007 Suresh Banarse. All rights reserved.

No part of this book may be reproduced, stored in a retrieval system, or transmitted by any means without the written permission of the author.

First published by AuthorHouse 3/19/2007

ISBN: 978-1-4259-9336-8 (sc)

Printed in the United States of America
Bloomington, Indiana

This book is printed on acid-free paper.

Dedicated to all of my family, you have inspired me to become the person I am.

Dedicated to my good friends, you have always had faith in me.

You are all truly exceptional.

Contents

Foreword ix

Introduction... xi

The Retail Model 1

Recruitment 15

Training..23

Coaching 31

Performance Management....................................39

Setting Objectives 47

Some Final Thoughts 57

Foreword

In an industry that continues to grow and attract talented people every day, these same people will often find themselves struggling for self direction and focusing their hard work on areas that just won't make a difference.

Every good Retail Manager will tell you how important planning and reviewing business progress is, they will tell you what an important role structure and consistency plays in their business.

The exceptional Retail Managers who I come across every day in my life tell me how important it is to clear the fog from around their people, giving them clarity. They tell me how important it is to show their people what to do, help them do it and then thank them.

Even at a senior level the essentials remain the same and the people who shine in retail management are the ones who don't forget that. These are the people who get to know their staff and enable them to grow. These are the people who show their staff what they need to do to reach acceptable, good and exceptional standards. These are the people who exceed company expectations and deliver customer service that is second to none, time and time again.

To become exceptional in retail management you need passion, vision and a clear plan. To become an exceptional Retail Manager you need to share this plan with your people and get them on board. If you treat them exceptionally and make them exceptional you will become an exceptional Retail Manager.

Malcolm Knight
Chartered FCIPD

Introduction

The retail business employs millions of people across the UK. In a lifetime many people will have some experience of working in retail, some will love it and others will hate it.

Everyone has to shop, and its no secret that whilst some people love shopping, others hate it. Whatever side of this love hate divide people fall into, everyone prefers to spend shopping time in a place where they have a good shopping experience.

And that's where you fit in.

**Whatever sector of retail you work in,
it's in your interest to make your customers'
shopping experience a good one.**

If you do everything in your power to impress your customers, most of them will come back to your shop, or recommend it to someone else.

If you don't, they will only come back if they have to and will tell people not to shop there.

Aside from price, the two things that will impress your customers are service and standards.

If you don't get it right you can be sure your competitors will.

People talk about the secrets behind good stores, good managers and good performance indicators; most of them make perfect sense.

There are however, some basic facts that will drive excellent performance and make you an exceptional Retail Manager.

A successful retail outlet needs:

- A quality saleable product

  Something that will be bought at a reasonably competitive price, this book assumes you have that product in the sector of retail that you work in.

- Good people

  This means well trained people who understand what they need to do and who take ownership in your business. A well trained, enthusiastic member of staff will drive your business. A poorly trained, de-motivated member of staff will damage your business.

- Complete Customer Focus

  Your people need to know their customers' needs and make the shopping experience enjoyable for them. Your people need to know what excellent customer service looks like.

MOST IMPORTANTLY IT NEEDS YOU

You Set the Standard

Your retail business needs a figurehead, someone who motivates, guides, sets goals, targets, rewards and recognises. It needs a leader who is a role model, and is not afraid to encourage and embrace change.

As businesses evolve, their people have to change their ways of working. Managers need to enhance the skill sets of their staff and prepare them for new competition and challenges.

An exceptional Retail Manager will drive that change and position themselves to develop their business through the people they work with, setting standards with them and helping them achieve those standards.

Behaviour Breeds Behaviour

For years people have said that Behaviour Breeds Behaviour, and it's true. Your staff will take their lead from you. If you go into different branches of multiple retail chains you will experience different levels of service.

At the end of the day, the level of service that you receive is dictated by the Manager in that outlet. And remember, if you are not offering excellent customer service, you are losing money and valuable profit.

If you strive to be an exceptional Retail Manager your people will become exceptional too.

This book will give you some simple tools, based on a straightforward model, the Retail Model, to help you get the most from your people.

Not so many radical ideas, but lots of common sense and practical tips, based on experience that will enable you to drive your business and be an exceptional Retail Manager.

At the end of the day retail is about selling things and how best you can do that with the resources that you have. Used properly this book will guide you, and ensure you are doing everything you can with the people who work for you.

This book offers you structure and focused support, because we all know the retail environment is fast paced and hectic. It will give you an overview of some of the key focus areas in retail which drive exceptional performance. It will help you develop your retail outlet into a shop of choice for your customers.

xiv

The Retail Model

The Retail Model is designed to be used in three ways.

Assess and Review your existing staff

- Look at all of your key members of staff and understand where they are on the model and what actions you should be taking with them. Review them against this model on a regular basis.

Use it with New Staff

- Use it during the recruitment process, structuring timelines for development and measuring performance around the model.

Teach Your Key Staff

- Make sure your key staff understand the model so that they can use it as a guide for developing the people that report into them. Teaching the model, and discussing performance around the model will give you a common language and a structure to use when discussing individuals' performance.

The rest of this chapter will introduce you to the Retail Model stage by stage and the rest of the chapters in this book will take you into more detail around the resources available to you at each stage of the model.

Suresh Banarse

RECRUIT

Effective recruitment will have a huge impact on your business

As a Retail Manager, when you recruit employees you need to be sure you are taking the right person on. Recruiting the right person to fill the right role will have a huge impact on your business. The chapter on recruitment later in this book will go into more detail on how to recruit, but for now, here are some key things that you need to consider.

- Have a clear idea of what the role is that you are recruiting for. Don't oversell it to try and fill it. This will end in expectations not being met and people leaving.

- Remember personality and attitude. Often someone with the right personality and attitude, but less hands on experience will out-perform someone with more experience, but the wrong personality and attitude.

- Make sure the person will fit in with the wider team. If they are working with other people, get them to meet informally. If they are reporting into someone other than you, involve this person at the recruitment stage. This will get their line manager's buy in to recruit the right person and help make the appointment successful.

The Exceptional Retail Manager

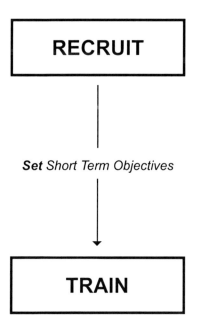

Good training will have a huge positive impact on your business.

Bad training will have just as big an impact, but it won't be positive.

Suresh Banarse

At this stage of the Retail Model, you need to make sure that you do two things for your new recruit

Set short term objectives

- Make these very clear, with timescales. Tell them what you want them to be doing in one week, two weeks and four weeks time. By setting objectives you are giving them clear direction and a clear understanding of your expectations. Specific methods for objective setting are discussed in a later chapter of this book.

Train them

- This training needs to cover all aspects of their job role. It needs to consider how much they already know and has to cover everything you set for them in their objectives.

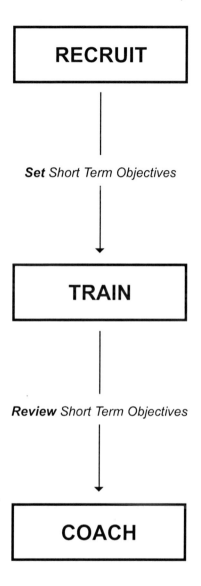

Once your staff member has been trained in the basic area of their job role, your role needs to start changing from trainer to coach.

Suresh Banarse

Training equips them with the skills they need to do their job; coaching lets them improve those skills.

It is common for new recruits at this stage to feel a bit de-motivated, because the initial excitement of taking on the job role has gone and reality is starting to sink in. At this stage, people understand what they need to do their job, your coaching will refine their skills and motivate them.

The Exceptional Retail Manager

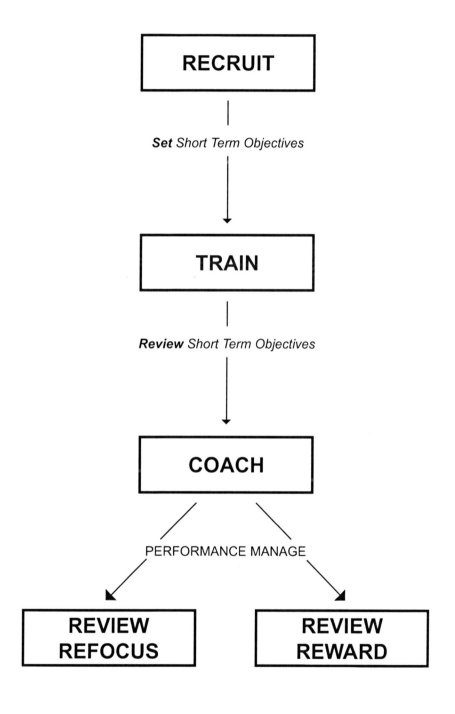

Suresh Banarse

Train, coach and regularly review your staff

If they are doing well and achieving the targets you have agreed, reward them. This doesn't have to be financial, it can be through praise, increased responsibility or even a good, documented review.

What's important here is that people know they are doing well and you encourage them to get better.

If they are not achieving the targets you set for them, they need refocusing. You need to understand where and why they are not achieving and give them the support they need to refocus.

The chapter on performance management will go into rewarding and refocusing in more detail.

The Retail Model - A common sense approach to business performance

The Retail Model

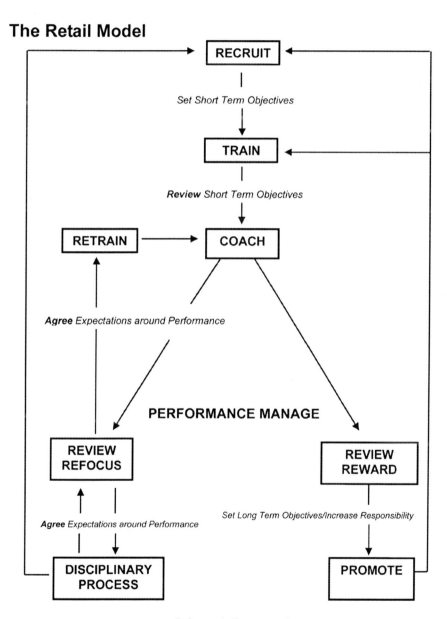

Suresh Banarse

If you find yourself continually reviewing and rewarding someone, on the right of the Retail Model, because they are achieving their objectives, there is a chance that it will end in promotion.

These people are motivated, increasing their experience and taking on increased responsibility. These are the people who are making your business a success. They understand what good looks like, and are achieving for you.

Remember, at some point these staff will need more training to support their development, so on the Retail Model, there is an arrow to train from promote.

It is inevitable that some may move on to bigger jobs in other businesses and when this happens we see an arrow from promote to recruit where you will need to take on new staff. The key here is contingency planning, so when it happens you have a back up.

On the left side of the model, if you are continually refocusing a member of staff you need to establish the following

- Are they getting the support they require from other people?

- Are they getting the training they need?

- Is there a problem with their capability or attitude?

Once you have investigated these three key areas, at some point you may need to take the matter down the disciplinary route. This tends to have one of three effects

The Exceptional Retail Manager

- It will give the person the wake up call they need to start performing;

- They will seek alternative employment;

- They will continue to under perform and you will eventually exit them from the business.

How does the model reflect what you do with your staff?

The key to its successful use is consistency.

There is a high chance that if you are passionate about your business you will use most aspects of the Retail Model already, without even thinking about it.

Using it consistently and fairly and getting others to do the same thing will help you develop keen, motivated, well trained people who will fulfil your expectations through excellent customer service and standards of work.

The rest of this book will go into some detail on specific areas of the model.

Recruitment

Getting the right people

Recruitment is one of the most important things you will do in your retail outlet. Recruit the right people and your business will improve.

Suresh Banarse

Think about each specific vacancy you have and ask yourself the following …

- What is the perfect fit candidate for that vacancy and why?

- Who was in that vacancy previously and where did they not perform?

- Who was in that vacancy previously and what did they do particularly well?

- What skills are you looking for in a new person to add value to your business?

- Is there anyone internally who you could develop into that role?

- Is there a danger that you might fill that vacancy with someone who does not suit it because you need a body?

If you are going to hire someone because you need a body and they don't fit the job specification, don't do it, you will struggle in the long run.

Either the person will leave because they are not suited to the vacancy or you will end up disciplining them because they are underperforming. Either way, it puts you right back to square one.

What makes exceptional Retail Managers stand out is the fact that they will wait and suffer to ensure they recruit the right people into the right places. This means in the long term, their retail outlet will benefit from strong, focused, well motivated people, who want to be in their jobs and therefore take pride in their work.

The Exceptional Retail Manager

How do you know who
the right person is?

The right people come in all sorts of shapes and sizes, and have all sorts of different skills.

The right person isn't a replica of who was in the job role before.

The right person isn't someone who can fit the shift pattern.

The right person isn't a replica of you.

The right person isn't necessarily someone who you get on with really well.

To understand who the right person is,
ask yourself the following;

- What are the specific tasks the person will have to carry out and therefore what is the skill base that you are looking for?

Now consider the following:

- What characteristics do you need that person to have to complement the team that you have in store?

- What transferable skills do you need that person to have; these may range from time management to supervisory skills?

Suresh Banarse

- What technical skills do you require that person to have to do the job?

- What skills will that person be able to develop on the job?

A large part of your decision needs to consider personality and attitude.

Unless you are recruiting for a very technical position that requires a very specific skill set you should be focusing in the following areas.

- **Motivation** – how self motivated is that person, and how much drive do they have?

- **Customer focus** – what does customer service mean to them, is it their number one priority?

- **Communication** – will that person communicate with customers, colleagues and line managers?

- **Teamwork** – will they work within a team or are they likely to go off and do their own thing?

Whilst there are other areas you need to consider, the above are essential to anyone who joins the retail business.

So how do you find all this out?

Ask very specific questions around these areas and ask for specific examples of what they have done in these areas. Ask

The Exceptional Retail Manager

situational questions, put them in scenarios that you are familiar with and ask how they would react.

Listen to what they say, and then ask yourself, do they reach the standard that you would expect?

If they do, focus on their technical skills and then make a decision, are they skilled enough or do they lack too much in specific skills areas.

Remember the Law

Get familiar with employment law and best practices. Age Discrimination, Equal Opportunities, Disability Discrimination, be aware of what you should and shouldn't ask in interviews and don't prejudge people. Remember the right person can come in all sorts of shapes and sizes.

Formulate a check list, one that works for you, that will tell you if the person you are interviewing will fit the vacancy that you have.

Training

The key to performance

Good training will make a massive difference in your retail outlet.

Suresh Banarse

Whether you are training someone new, training someone in a new skill or refresher training, the effort that you put into their training will impact the success you have in your store.

Put more simply, if someone knows how to do their job, they will do it properly. They will be confident, motivated and execute it to the standard that is required.

If someone doesn't know how to do their job, they will execute it poorly, be demoralised and have a negative impact on your business and the people around them.

Remember, behaviour breeds behaviour.

Too often, Retail Managers will bypass training by throwing people in at the deep end. Whilst this may work sometimes, it teaches people bad habits and is not a constructive way to teach people how to do their job properly.

So what should you train people on?

If you have new staff you should train them on all aspects of their job requirement and ensure they are fully competent in these areas.

For existing staff, train them on new initiatives and take them through refresher training on existing parts of their job role, because it doesn't take long for people to forget or slip into bad ways. If they are under performing on specific aspects of their job, retrain them in those areas.

The Exceptional Retail Manager

Planned, structured, all encompassing training in your retail outlet will provide you with high standards and consistency across your store.

It will also mean that your staff know how and why they should comply with your particular policies and procedures.

How should you train?

Here are some guidelines that you should follow to offer your staff effective training.

Ask questions

- Ask them about specific areas that you are going to train them in. This will give you a good idea of how much they know and let you pitch your training at the right level. If you pitch it too high, they will learn very little and become de-motivated. If you pitch it too low, they will learn nothing and may get frustrated or feel patronised.

- Don't assume that people know things already, as you may miss out important bits of their training.

- Ask questions once you have started training them, to get them to show you that they understand.

Prepare to Train

- Know what you are going to train them on and why. If possible offer them different ways of training, as people respond differently to different methods of training.

Plan the training

- Don't rush it, don't cram it into unrealistic time frames. Break it into bits and train them on a piece at a time, ensuring they understand each one of those pieces.

- Plan what you are going to use to train them and how you are going to follow it up after you have trained them.

Show them Good

- Let them see what they are aiming for, set the standard so that they are in no doubt as to what you want them to achieve. Then, map out the route with them, agreeing timescales.

Give them feedback

- During the training, make it honest and descriptive. Tell them exactly where they are not performing and also where they are. Congratulate them when they are doing well.

- Remember, something that is old hat to you is brand new and difficult for them.

Give them Context

- Tell them what the big picture is and why they need to do what they are doing. When you know why you are doing something it's easier to do.

Offer Different Learning Experiences

- Some people like to learn by reading, some by doing, some by watching. Understand that people have different learning

The Exceptional Retail Manager

styles and as far as possible offer them a range of ways to train.

If you don't train your staff,
they will not be able to do their job
and they will probably leave.

- In organisations which are heavily reliant on procedure, compliance and teamwork, poor training will have a negative knock on effect on individuals and ultimately the whole of your business.

- At the same time, good training will have a positive affect on your business, ensuring people comply, remain motivated and reach standards that you set them.

Coaching

Building their skills

What Is Coaching?

When you are training someone, you are teaching them a specific skill to allow them to do their job, you are giving them new skills.

When you coach someone, you are helping them to get better at using those skills that they have already been trained on.

Think about sportspeople, they know how to play their sport, they know the rules and what they have to do to succeed in their game.

They get better at how they play their game through coaching, by taking advice from other people, considering different ways of doing things and by practising.

Think about when you first learned to ride a bike.

Before you could get really good at it, you had to learn how to do it. You had to learn to balance, peddle and look ahead all at the same time.

Once you listened to other people's ideas, watched how they did it, tried different ways and got some encouragement, you got better and better.

Now you ride a bike without even thinking and probably coach other people to ride theirs.

Suresh Banarse

How do you Coach?

There are two types of coaching, formal and informal. Both are relevant to retail, both will help your people develop and both should be happening in your business.

Many good theories have been developed to help people coach, some of them simple and some very in-depth. All these theories have common areas which are summarised here. Focus on these and they will help you coach your staff.

Formal Coaching

- Set aside quality time to spend with staff to observe and assess their performance.

- Understand the areas where their skills need improving by observing and asking questions.

- Ensure that you and they agree these are the areas where they need coaching.

- Ask them what they think they can do to improve their performance, listen to what they tell you and suggest some ideas of your own.

- Don't tell them outright, try and get them to tell you.

Formal Coaching

- Discuss the pros and cons of these ideas, don't shun their ideas in favour of yours, praise and recognise their input.

The Exceptional Retail Manager

- Agree what the next level of performance looks like and how and when they should be aiming to get there. Be sure to discuss the increasingly positive impact this will have on your business and on the people around them.

- Praise them for the work they have put in so far, inspire them to reach the next level and motivate them to remain focused.

- Agree actions and action plans, document these together and make sure they are in line with any objectives you may have set them already.

Informal Coaching

As the name suggests, has less structure than formal coaching. It can be done anytime or anyplace and is often the result of you observing someone doing something at work that you know a better way of doing.

To make it effective, there are some guidelines you should follow to coach informally.

If you approach it wrong, you can come across as patronising, aggressive or even arrogant and this will do your business no favours in the long run.

Informal Coaching

- Approach the subject positively; tell the person what was good about what you just saw them do.

35

Suresh Banarse

- Ask them if they have seen the task completed any other way and listen to their answer. Then suggest an alternative way of completing the task, encouraging their input and praising any ideas they may have.

- Explain the benefits of alternative methods to them, sell it to them. Tell them how it will help them and make their work easier. If relevant, tell them how it will benefit other people around them, give them context.

- Ask them to have a try and check that they understand how you want them to try it by showing them and getting them to repeat it, if possible.

- Ask the person what they think of the idea, tell them to come and ask if they have any other ideas on how to do the task.

- Finish on a positive, - praise, encourage and motivate

Key Coaching Behaviours

Whether formal or informal, there are some key behaviours you need to be using.

A Positive Outlook

Praising what people have done and inspiring them to achieve more will improve your people, your standards and your profit margin.

The Exceptional Retail Manager

A good coach and exceptional Retail Manager, who understands this, will motivate people at all levels of their business to ensure they are constantly developing their skills.

Good Questioning and Listening Techniques

To understand where people need coaching you need to know how to gather information from them.

- **Open Questions** – generally starting with Who, What, Why, When or How will let you gather specific information from them and ensure that they get an opportunity to put over their point of view.

- **Closed questions**—are ones that just have yes or no answers. When you use too many of these, opportunities to express ideas or concerns is limited and your coaching session may focus in the wrong area.

A selection of open questions to gather information and closed questions to narrow that information down will make sure you are tackling the right areas with individuals.

And when you've asked questions, listen to the answers.

Don't just listen to the bits that you want to hear, actively listen to everything that they are saying to you and make sure they know you are listening.

Suresh Banarse

If you don't listen to people,
eventually they will stop talking to you.

Feedback

- A good coach gives specific, relevant feedback. They will make the feedback constructive and focus on good areas as well as the development areas of the individual.

- Without feedback, people don't know how they are doing and with unstructured feedback, they will get demoralised.

Try the sandwich technique, a method that has been used for many years …

POSITIVE

Start on something they are doing well.

CONSTRUCTIVE

Bring in the area that you feel they can do differently.

POSITIVE

Finish on a high, reaffirming good performance and praising.

Performance Management

Staying on track

Managing performance effectively will impact every area of your business.

As the name suggests, performance management, put simply, is a process which lets you manage how your business performs.

To manage your business well, and to get exceptional results, you need to invest time and effort into the management of your people.

Ultimately to manage the performance of your business, you have to manage the performance of your people.

Performance Management helps you get the best out of individuals.

Performance Management is about communicating, understanding, agreeing and documenting the following with all of your staff regularly:

- Their objectives

- Performance against objectives

- Performance against expectations

- Performance as part of the team.

Suresh Banarse

To be a good performance manager there are fundamentals that you need to make sure you do.

- **Set** and agree objectives

- **Review** objectives regularly

- **Train** and coach to enable people to accomplish their objectives

- **Feedback** performance in one to ones and get their understanding of how they feel they are doing

- **Motivate** and encourage people to perform every day

- **Be Honest** and constructive in any performance related discussion.

Follow these key steps with your staff and you will find yourself spending more time rewarding and praising, rather than refocusing, disciplining and recruiting for vacancies.

An exceptional Retail Manager will create a work environment where people will want to perform, by investing time and structure in the development and monitoring of those people.

A retail business which has an effective performance management system in place encourages the following:

Fairness

- All employees are treated the same. There is no special treatment and there are no favourites.

The Exceptional Retail Manager

Motivation

- People are inspired to perform as they are encouraged and praised by their line managers, understand what they have achieved and what they need to achieve.

Opportunity

- Regular reviews, feedback and discussion will highlight development areas for people and opportunities for increased responsibility and promotion.

Teamwork

- In a positive work environment, where people are clear on what they need to achieve, and where they fit into the bigger picture, your employees will bond as a team supporting each other.

Communication

- Not only between you and your employees, but between employees and their peers. An open, constructive work environment encourages people to raise concerns and discuss issues, whether personal or business.

A good performance management system in a retail environment focuses on under, over and steady performance.

An exceptional Retail Manager will pay as much attention to all three areas. Following the steps listed in this chapter will create

Suresh Banarse

an environment which lets you maximise the performance of your business.

In the majority of cases you will be managing people's performance upwards, helping them to develop new skills and take on more responsibility.

In circumstances where people are consistently under performing you need to make sure you have covered the following areas:

- Are they getting the support and training they need?

- Is the issue capability or attitude?

- Do they understand what your expectations are?

In retail, we will always lose people who under perform. The very nature of retail means we can not afford to tolerate persistent underperformance.

Its impact on the team, your standards and your customer experience can be very bad, but remember, this is only a small part of the performance management process.

An exceptional Retail Manager is not afraid to be 100% honest about people's performance.

The Exceptional Retail Manager

A well implemented performance management process in your store will ensure you are doing everything you can to develop your people and your business.

Setting Objectives

Creating an End Goal

Objectives give you a structured way to make your staff aware of what they need to do.

- **They don't** have to be complicated, in-depth or full of jargon.

- **They do** need to reflect what you have to achieve in your business.

To make objectives effective they need to be S.M.A.R.T. *

S – Specific – Be very specific about exactly what it is that you want people to achieve, don't leave any room for misinterpretation.

M – Measurable – Make sure there is a way to measure progress against this objective.

A – Achievable – Will they be able to achieve them, is support available?

R - Realistic – Will they be able to achieve this task, have they got the resource and the support that they need?

T – Timed - Set timescales for each area of the objective and agree these timescales, set timescales for reviews as well.

*SMART is a generic, widely adopted model used across many industries and educational establishments.

Suresh Banarse

How do you create objectives?

The template overleaf, gives you a simple structure to create useable objectives with your staff, whatever level of your business they are in.

The same template will give you a lot of personal focus if you use it to write objectives that reflect your workload.

Objective Setting Template				
Desired Output	Actions	Timescales	Measurement	Support Needed
What needs to be achieved	How it needs to be done	When it needs to be done	How you will measure progress	What support you will give your trainee

When should you set objectives?

The people in your business should be guided in almost everything they do by clear structured objectives.

If they are, they will know exactly what they need to be doing and aiming for in the future.

As your objectives are cascaded down to the people who work in your store they need to reflect what these people need to do

The Exceptional Retail Manager

in their job roles. If everyone who works for you achieves their objectives you will achieve yours.

Depending on who you are setting objectives with, you need to consider whether they need long or short term objectives or both.

Businesses lose most people in their first three months of employment. Much of the time this is because they lack clarity in what they are meant to be achieving and do not get the training they require. As a direct result, they get de-motivated and disillusioned and it is often easier for them to leave, rather than ask for support.

Refer back to the Retail Model. At the top, you have new starters. Here you will need objectives to cover their first couple of months and give them absolute clarity in what they need to do.

As these people move down the model they will need longer term objectives to guide and motivate them.

For staff on the left hand side of the Retail Model, you will need to agree short term objectives.

These staff are underperforming and need short term clarity on where they need to improve.

They should also have a good idea of what they need to achieve long term to give them context and an understanding of why they need to achieve their short term objectives.

51

Suresh Banarse

For staff on the right hand side of the Retail Model, these are your exceptional performers.

These people need to have long term objectives so that they understand where they are going to develop and how. You should also set short term objectives with them in areas where they are developing new skills.

Look overleaf for some example objectives.

Rudy is a new part time till operator and needs short term objectives to focus his training

Desired Output	Actions	Timescales	Measurement	Support Needed
Understand all cashier functions of the till	Read till handbook Observe cashier for two shifts	Immediately Week 1	Till checklist quiz Feedback from cashier and supervisor	To be scheduled with Tina in week one
Practice on till Serve customers under supervision	4 hours in training mode Conduct two shifts with supervisor observing	Week 1 Week 2	Feedback from trainer Feedback from supervisor and accuracy of till	Training till Availability of supervisor for assistance
Go live on tills	Conduct shifts	Week 3 and 4	Accuracy of tills, customer feedback, supervisor feedback	Support from other operators and scheduling at non peak times

The Exceptional Retail Manager

Kalika works in grocery, there have been issues with her standards, rotation of stock and backup areas

Desired Output	Actions	Timescales	Measurement	Support Needed
Shelves faced and filled to agreed standard every shift	Agree acceptable standard with duty manager Check back up area for old stock at start of every shift	Immediately and ongoing	Feedback from duty manager Feedback from morning shift Clearance of backup stock	Time with duty manager Help to initially reorganise and label back up area
Back up to reduce in stockholding by at least half	Review back stock at start of shift Discuss over ordering issues with duty manager immediately	Within 4 weeks As and when this occurs	Back up area Inventory figures	Continued support from duty manager to avoid over ordering Less time covering till

Maya has been with you for two months, you are giving her focus for the next 6 months

Desired Output	Actions	Timescales	Measurement	Support Needed
Become a duty manager and run weekend shifts	Shadow all duty managers at least once Complete duty management workbook and present project to senior team	2 months 6 months	Feedback from duty managers Feedback from mentor	Get scheduled on rota for relevant shifts Mentor to be assigned
Enhance profile with rest of store team	Run two staff briefings	Within 2 months	Feedback from staff and line manager	Briefing packs from head office and training on how to use them

Suresh Banarse

OBJECTIVES MOTIVATE

When people can see what they have achieved by reviewing their objectives they will be motivated and proud of what they have achieved. For many people, reviewing objectives is a way to self measure and self motivate.

- Achieving their objectives inspires them to step up to the next level and continue to achieve.

- Reviewing objectives regularly lets you measure, refocus and reward people.

- Achieving objectives will let your staff see how their skills have developed and will encourage career progression.

- Seeing your staff achieve their objectives will motivate you.

If people don't have objectives they will lack focus. Their achievements will go unrecognised and they may be misguided in their daily actions. Ultimately this may harm your business and you will lose good staff

An exceptional Retail Manager will have clear personal objectives that tie into their business plan.

An exceptional Retail Manager will cascade their objectives to the key people in their business.

An exceptional Retail Manager will be flexible with objectives to accommodate any changes in the direction or focus of their business.

The Exceptional Retail Manager

SMART objectives will help you in your quest to have well trained, motivated staff, displaying consistently high standards and offering high levels of customer service.

Some Final Thoughts

Retail Management is hard work but very rewarding.

There's a lot to do, often with limited resources. When things go wrong, they can have knock on effects on the whole of your business and the people who work in it. When they go right, the effect can be extremely motivational and positive.

Retail is full of dedicated, passionate people who enjoy interacting with customers and achieving high standards. If this doesn't reflect the staff in your store, you need to understand why not.

The key to being an exceptional Retail Manager is to have structure in what you do, and consistency in your approach to your business through your people.

Be realistic with what you want to achieve and be realistic in what you think your staff are able to achieve. At the same time don't hold back, stretch yourself and your staff, because that stimulates self development.

Be structured in how you plan your time and the time of your key staff. Have a good understanding of what your staff are focusing on and why, remember what they do needs to achieve your objectives and tie into your business plan.

Be aware of how your people are feeling, are they motivated, are they challenged, or are they feeling stressed? Address any issues before they get out of proportion.

Create a training and coaching culture in your store. Make your store a place where your staff want to learn and teach, where they want to help each other and the business to develop.

Ask yourself everyday ...

Is my customer service unrivalled?

Are my standards unrivalled?

If the answer is no, you are compromising and settling for second best, you need to understand why.

Using the Retail Model will help to give you a structure that will focus your business in the places that make a difference.

Practise what you preach.

Remember, behaviour breeds behaviour, you set the standard and you decide when the standard isn't being reached.

An exceptional Retail Manager is one who takes immediate action to rectify issues and puts long term plans in place to stop them happening again.

Be exceptional in your approach to your staff and you will become an exceptional Retail Manager.

About the Author

Suresh Banarse started his retail life working with his family on their market stalls in Petticoat Lane and Portabella Road. His first move into big business saw him join the hospitality industry working in central London.

From here he ventured into the retail business where he has worked in Operations and Human Resource positions for fifteen years.

Suresh is currently Head of Training and Recruitment for an international high street retailer. His focus is around driving development and performance of people at all levels of the business, encouraging personal development, enabling business growth and encouraging internal promotions.

To contact the author send an email to exceptionalretail@yahoo.co.uk